SAINT JOHN PAUL II: A PILGRIM IN IRELAND

G000039805

BISHOP DONAL MURRAY

Saint John Paul II
A Pilgrim in Ireland

VERITAS

First published 2014 by
Veritas Publications
7–8 Lower Abbey Street
Dublin 1
publications@veritas.ie
www.veritas.ie

ISBN 978 1 84730 556 5

10 9 8 7 6 5 4 3 2 1

A catalogue record for this book is available
from the British Library.

Cover design by Lir Mac Cárthaigh, Veritas Publications
Cover image: Pope John Paul II celebrates Mass in Knock, Ireland 1979.
© Tim Graham/CORBIS
Printed in the Republic of Ireland by Hudson Killeen Ltd, Dublin

*Veritas books are printed on paper made from the wood pulp
of managed forests. For every tree felled, at least one tree is planted,
thereby renewing natural resources.*

CONTENTS

INTRODUCTION

To say that Karol Wojtyla's early life was eventful would be an understatement. He was born on 18 May 1920, just as Polish independence had been regained after more than a century. He was the youngest of a loving family, but by the time he was twelve all of his immediate family, with the exception of his father, had died. A sister died before he was born, his mother before he was ten and his elder brother, a doctor, when he was twelve.

At the age of twenty his world, and all his expectations, collapsed. Polish independence was lost and the country came under Nazi occupation. Shortly after that, his father died. Karol found work in a quarry and later in a chemical factory. His young life had been marked by sadness, hardship and danger.

His preparation for the priesthood began in the occupied city of Krakow in 1942, initially while he continued to work in the factory. Shortly after the end of the war he was ordained to the priesthood. He was sent to study at the Angelicum University in Rome. On his return to Poland, Karol taught in the Catholic University in Krakow and later in the University of Lublin. At the early age of thirty-eight he became Auxiliary Bishop of Krakow. During the Second Vatican Council he was named Archbishop of Krakow. He made a significant contribution to the preparatory work on the document *Gaudium et Spes*, a document that broke new ground by its focus on the relationship between the Church and the world.

On 16 October 1978, at the age of fifty-eight, Karol Wojtyla was elected pope. Looking back over his life with all its unexpected turns and often painful experiences, he could see God's call making itself heard at every step. When he returned as newly elected pope to his home town of Wadowice, he said:

> When in thought I look back over the long path of my life, I reflect on how the surroundings, the parish and my family *brought me to the baptismal font* of the church of Wadowice, where I was given on 20 June 1920 the grace to become a son of God, together with faith in my Redeemer. I have already solemnly kissed this font … when I

was Archbishop of Krakow. Today I wish to kiss it again as pope, successor of St Peter.[1]

Later, he wrote about the significance of Baptism:

> All vocations are born in Christ, and this is what is expressed by every anointing with Chrism – from holy Baptism to the anointing of the head of a bishop. This is the source of the dignity common to all Christian vocations, which, from this point of view, are all equal … Great care should be taken so that 'nothing is wasted' (Jn 6:12); no vocation should be wasted because all are valuable and necessary.[2]

---

[1] Words spoken in the parish church of Wadowice, 7 June 1979.
[2] John Paul II, *Rise, Let Us Be On Our Way* (London: Jonathan Cape, 2004), p. 37.

THE VISIT TO IRELAND
DUBLIN AND DROGHEDA
29 September 1979

Pope John Paul II's return to Poland was the second pastoral visit that he made outside Italy. The third was to Ireland. During that whirlwind visit, involving addresses to twenty-two different groups in a little over two days, he opened up many of the topics which were to become themes of his pontificate.

His first homily in Ireland, like his last encyclical, was about the mystery of the Eucharist. He remarked on the many different contexts in which the Mass was celebrated throughout Irish history:

> As I stand here, in the company of so many hundreds of thousands of Irish men and women, I am thinking of how many times, across how many centuries, the Eucharist has been celebrated in this

land. How many and how varied the places where Mass has been offered – in stately medieval and in splendid modern cathedrals; in early monastic and in modern churches; at Mass rocks in the glens and forests by 'hunted priests', and in poor thatch-covered chapels, for a people poor in worldly goods but rich in the things of the spirit, in 'wake-houses' or 'station houses', or at great open-air hostings of faithful – on the top of Croagh Patrick and at Lough Derg. Small matter where the Mass was offered; for the Irish, it was always the Mass that mattered.[3]

In his last encyclical he made a similar reflection on the many different contexts in which he had celebrated Mass, from great basilicas to lake shores, from altars erected in vast football stadiums, to the parish church where he had his first pastoral assignment. In that wide variety of locations he recognised what he called the cosmic character of the Eucharist which, whatever the particular context, is 'always celebrated on the altar of the world'.[4]

What lesson might these thoughts have for us? The Eucharist is celebrated in a great variety of local

---

[3] Homily, Phoenix Park, 29 September 1979. All homilies and messages, unless otherwise stated, can be found at www.vatican.va.
[4] Cf. John Paul II, *Ecclesia de Eucharistia*, 8. All encyclicals cited can be found at www.vatican.va.

communities; it gathers the people of a particular place, their families with their memories, hopes, sorrows, anxieties and gifts.

But in doing so we become part of something greater, something universal. What is offered in the Mass is the Body of Christ, who, as he promised, is drawing all things to himself. All creation is being drawn into his offering of himself on Calvary and into his entry into the new creation. All those present seek to join their whole lives in that offering and in that transformation. Throughout his years as pope he often returned to the theme of Eucharist with which he began his visit to Ireland.[5]

The Eucharist is the highest expression of the unique role of the human family – the only part of the earthly creation that can freely and consciously praise its Creator:

> Through the human person, spokesperson for all creation, all living things praise the Lord. Our breath of life that also presupposes self-knowledge, awareness and freedom becomes the song and prayer of the whole of life that vibrates in the universe.[6]

[5] Cf. also *Mane Nobiscum Domine* (for the Year of the Eucharist, 2004–2005): *Dies Domini* (On the Lord's Day); *Vicesimus Quintus Annus* (on the 20th Anniversary of the Liturgy Constitution of Vatican II).
[6] John Paul II, General Audience, 9 January 2002.

Later that day of 29 September, Pope John Paul visited Drogheda. His themes included Ireland's long history of fidelity to the faith preached by St Patrick. Ireland, he said, 'has been a Church of martyrs, a Church of witnesses, a Church of heroic faith, heroic fidelity'.[7] The particular challenge he issued in Drogheda was that of building peace. Peace must be based on justice, that is, on the dignity of the human being in the light of the Gospel. This had been the topic of his first encyclical.[8] The second basis is to recognise that peace cannot be built on violence. The third is reconciliation:

> Communities who stand together in their acceptance of Jesus' supreme message of love, expressed in peace and reconciliation, and in their rejection of all violence, constitute an irresistible force for achieving what many have come to accept as impossible and destined to remain so.[9]

The reference to what people accept as impossible takes on a new significance in the light of the unexpected fall of the Iron Curtain, to which he contributed by his peaceful but insistent call for justice and freedom. Some years

---

[7] Homily, Drogheda, 29 September 1979.
[8] Cf. John Paul II, *Redemptor Hominis*, 4 March 1979.
[9] Homily, Drogheda, 29 September 1979.

before he had spoken about the social evil that springs from the sin of 'those who take refuge in the supposed impossibility of changing the world'.[10]

A neglected source of his later teaching on issues of justice, peace and reconciliation is the series of messages that he issued in each year of his pontificate for the World Day of Peace.[11]

---

[10] John Paul II, *Reconciliatio et Paenitentia*, 16.
[11] http://www.vatican.va/holy_father/john_paul_ii/messages/peace/index.htm.

GALWAY AND KNOCK
30 September 1979

For many people, the most memorable moment of the papal visit was the Mass celebrated for the youth of Ireland in Galway. John Paul's address was full of praise and encouragement, of recognition of the importance of the role that belonged to his young audience: 'Tomorrow Ireland will depend on you.' But his words did not underestimate the challenges that awaited them. Thirty-five years later, after those young people have lived through the folly of the Celtic Tiger, the pope's words ring all too true:

> The more you possess – you may be tempted to think – the more you will feel liberated from every type of confinement. In order to make more money and to possess more, in order to eliminate effort and worry, you may be tempted to take moral

shortcuts where honesty, truth and work are concerned … Mass media, entertainment and literature will present a model for living where all too often it is every man for himself, and where the unrestrained affirmation of self leaves no room for concern for others … A society that, in this way, has lost its higher religious and moral principles will become an easy prey for manipulation and for domination by the forces which, under the pretext of greater freedom, will enslave it ever more.[12]

He went on to say:

Something else is needed: something that you will find only in Christ, for he alone is the measure and the scale that you must use to evaluate your own life. In Christ you will discover the true greatness of your own humanity; he will make you understand your own dignity as human beings 'created to the image and likeness of God'.[13]

It may not be too fanciful to suggest that this gathering in Galway sowed the seeds of what grew into the celebration of World Youth Day. The international World Youth Day

---

[12] Homily, Galway, 30 September 1979.
[13] Ibid.

takes place every two or three years and around a million young people attend. On some occasions there have been many more; there were an estimated five million present in Manila in 1995.

At his final encounter in Toronto in 2002, Pope John Paul explained what led him to call the first World Youth Day in 1985:

> I imagined the World Youth Days as a *powerful moment* in which the young people of the world could meet Christ, who is eternally young, and could learn from him how to be *bearers of the Gospel to other young people*.[14]

The pope began his homily in Knock with the words, 'Here I am at the goal of my journey to Ireland'. Already in the first year of his pontificate he had visited the shrines of Our Lady of Graces outside Rome, Guadalupe, Jasna Góra and Loreto. In doing so, he expressed both his devotion to the Blessed Virgin and the importance of places of pilgrimage:

---

[14] Vigil with Young People, Toronto, 27 July 2002 (italics in original).

I know very well that every people, every country, indeed every diocese, has its *holy places* in which *the heart of the whole people of God beats, one could say, in more lively fashion*: places of special encounter between God and human beings; places in which Christ dwells in a special way in our midst.[15]

But we live in a changing world, and remaining faithful to our long tradition of faith and mission makes new demands all the time:

> Every generation, with its own mentality and characteristics, is like a new continent to be won for Christ. The Church must constantly look for new ways that will enable her to understand more profoundly and to carry out with renewed vigour the mission received from her Founder.[16]

---

[15] Homily, Knock, 30 September 1979 (italics in original). At the end of 2001, the Holy See published the Directory on Popular Piety. Pope Francis pointed to the value of traditional expressions of faith in *Evangelii Gaudium,* 122–126.

[16] The evangelising of changing cultures is also mentioned in the document on catechesis *Catechesi Tradendae,* published two weeks after his return from Ireland, and in an important passage in *Centesimus Annus,* 24. At the heart of every culture, he says, is the attitude people take to the mystery of God.

The focus brought by Vatican II on the fact that every Christian community, every baptised person is, by definition, missionary was a constant element in the teaching of Pope John Paul II.[17] So too was his insistence on the need to bring the Gospel into the heart of a changing culture.

---

[17] Cf. especially *Redemptoris Missio*.

MAYNOOTH AND LIMERICK
1 October 1979

During his final hours in Ireland John Paul II met seminarians and then priests, missionaries and religious in Maynooth. He then met the last big gathering of his visit in Limerick. In both cases, the challenge spoken in Knock was made even more explicit. In Maynooth he said:

> You must work with the conviction that this generation, this decade of the 1980s which we are about to enter, could be crucial and decisive for the future of the faith in Ireland. Let there be no complacency.[18]

---

[18] Speech to Priests and Religious in Maynooth, 1 October 1979 (available at http://www.maynoothcollege.ie/news/AddressofHisHolinessPope JohnPaulIItoPriestsMissionariesReligiousBrothersandSistersatM.shtml).

At the same time he called them to be courageous and to 'work with confidence; work with joy. You are witnesses to the Resurrection of Christ'. He told the seminarians not to set their sights too low. The faith in Ireland today is linked to the fidelity of St Patrick, he told them, and 'tomorrow some part of God's plan will be linked to your fidelity'.

He also recognised that Maynooth had formed priests who ministered in every part of the world, and it had given birth in the twentieth century to two new missionary societies – the Columban Fathers and the Kiltegan Fathers. The Irish missionary outreach occurred all through Christian history, for instance:

> In the ninth and tenth centuries, Irish monks rekindled the light of faith in regions where it had burnt low or been extinguished by the collapse of the Roman Empire, and evangelised new nations not yet evangelised, including areas of my own native Poland.[19]

---

[19] Ibid.

In Limerick he spoke about the 'special dignity and mission entrusted to the lay people in the Church'. There is no such thing as an ordinary layperson, he said: 'Sometimes, lay men and women do not seem to appreciate to the full the dignity and the vocation that is theirs as lay people.'[20]

The particular spheres in which lay people have their mission are those in which they live and work, whether it is politics or media, education or whatever. All of these are part of the 'new continent',[21] because all bring up new questions on which the Gospel needs to be brought to bear. Every baptised person is called by Baptism to fulfil his or her role in bringing the Gospel to the world. This is a topic to which Pope John Paul frequently returned, most notably in the document on the vocation and mission of the laity.[22] He went on to state in the strongest terms that 'Ireland must choose ... This generation is once more a generation of decision.'[23]

---

[20] Homily, Limerick, 1 October 1979.
[21] Homily, Knock, 30 September 1979.
[22] John Paul II, *Christifideles Laici*, 23; cf. also *Laborem Exercens*, 27; cf. *Mulieris Dignitatem*.
[23] Homily, Limerick.

THE LONG PONTIFICATE

Pope John Paul II was to reign for twenty-six and a half years, probably the third longest pontificate in history. Among the most striking events were the assassination attempt on 13 May 1981, his visit to the Great Synagogue in Rome on 13 April 1986, the celebration of the Great Jubilee of the year 2000, and the publication of the *Catechism of the Catholic Church*.

No pope has ever spoken directly to so many people. In the course of his pontificate he conducted almost 1,200 General Audiences, attended by nearly eighteen million people. He visited 129 different countries on 104 foreign journeys. On World Youth Days, unforgettable experiences for those privileged to be present, millions of young people were inspired by him. He made nearly nine hundred visits to various places in Italy, including over three hundred visits to parishes in the Diocese of Rome.

His writings are a treasury from which the Church will draw for a long time to come. In particular, his encyclicals have given us rich reflections on Christ the Redeemer, on the Father of Mercies and on the Holy Spirit, Lord and Giver of Life.[24] He addressed major issues of social concern and the principles of the Church's social teaching.[25] He pointed with increasing insistence to the danger of losing sight of the human capacity to seek and discover the truth, and to how profoundly dehumanising that would be, especially in the sphere of morality.[26] In all of this we saw the passionate commitment to human dignity and freedom in every moment and condition of life that was expressed in his first encyclical. If we look at ourselves in the light of the Incarnation and Redemption, he said, this bears fruit not only of adoration of God but of wonder at ourselves: 'the name for that deep amazement at human worth and dignity is the Gospel.'[27]

His devotion to the Blessed Virgin was always clear. It was expressed in his visits to Marian shrines and in his encyclical *Redemptoris Mater* and his Apostolic Letter *Rosarium Virginis Mariae*.

---

[24] *Redemptor Hominis, Dives in Misericordia, Dominum et Vivificantem*.
[25] *Laborem Exercens, Sollicitudo Rei Socialis, Centesimus Annus*. He also had published the *Compendium of the Social Doctrine of the Church*.
[26] Especially in *Fides et Ratio, Veritatis Splendor* and *Evangelium Vitae*.
[27] John Paul II, *Redemptor Hominis*, 10.

Near the end of his long life, he sat, frail and ill, before a crowd of over three quarters of a million young people at the closing Mass of World Youth Day in Toronto, 2002. He looked back on his Christian life which began at the baptismal font of Wadowice:

> You are young, and the pope is old, eighty-two or eighty-three years of life is not the same as twenty-two or twenty-three. But the pope still fully identifies with your hopes and aspirations. Although I have lived through much darkness, under harsh totalitarian regimes, I have seen enough evidence to be unshakably convinced that no difficulty, no fear is so great that it can completely suffocate the hope that springs eternal in the hearts of the young.[28]

He was beatified by his successor, Pope Benedict XVI, on 1 May, Divine Mercy Sunday, 2011. On Divine Mercy Sunday, 27 April 2014, he was canonised together with Blessed John XXIII, the pope who summoned the Second Vatican Council. Pope John Paul II saw the Council as 'the great grace bestowed on the Church in the twentieth

---

[28] Homily, Closing Mass of World Youth Day, Toronto, 27 July 2002.

century: there we find a sure compass by which to take our bearings in the century now beginning'.[29]

[29] John Paul II, *Novo Millennio Ineunte*, 57.